Katharina Walter

Englisch an Stationen

Übungsmaterial zu den Kernthemen der Bildungsstandards **Klasse 5**

Auer Verlag

Die Herausgeber:

Marco Bettner: Rektor als Ausbildungsleiter, Haupt- und Realschullehrer, Referent in der Lehrerfort- und Lehrerweiterbildung

Dr. Erik Dinges: Rektor einer Förderschule für Lernhilfe, Referent in der Lehrerfort- und Lehrerweiterbildung

Die Autorin:

Katharina Walter: Fachlehrerin für Englisch und Französisch in der Sekundarstufe I

Gedruckt auf umweltbewusst gefertigtem, chlorfrei gebleichtem
und alterungsbeständigem Papier.

3. Auflage 2013
Nach den seit 2006 amtlich gültigen Regelungen der Rechtschreibung
© Auer Verlag
AAP Lehrerfachverlage GmbH, Donauwörth
Alle Rechte vorbehalten
Das Werk und seine Teile sind urheberrechtlich geschützt. Jede Nutzung in anderen als den gesetzlich zugelassenen Fällen bedarf der vorherigen schriftlichen Einwilligung des Verlages. Hinweis zu § 52a UrhG: Weder das Werk noch seine Teile dürfen ohne eine solche Einwilligung eingescannt und in ein Netzwerk eingestellt werden. Dies gilt auch für Intranets von Schulen und sonstigen Bildungseinrichtungen.
Illustrationen: Stefanie Aufmuth, Corinna Beurenmeister, Hendrik Kranenberg, Bettina Weyland
Satz: krauß-verlagsservice, Augsburg
Druck und Bindung: Franz X. Stückle Druck und Verlag, Ettenheim
ISBN 978-3-403-**06588**-3

www.auer-verlag.de

Inhaltsverzeichnis

Vorwort 5

Materialaufstellung und Hinweise zu den einzelnen Stationen 6

Route card 9

At home (simple present)
Station 1: My day 10
Station 2: What we do on Saturdays 11
Station 3: We don't and he doesn't 12
Station 4: Do you like it? 13
Station 5: Are you happy? 14
Station 6: What I always do 15
Station 7: Family members 16
Station 8: About my family 17
Station 9: Relationships 18
Station 9: Cards 19
Station 10: I have got a nice room 20
Station 11: She hasn't got a sister 21
Station 12: Rooms 22
Station 13: Animals 23
Station 13: Domino cards 24
Station 14: Pets 25
Station 14: Cards 26

Sports and hobbies (present progressive)
Station 1: I am playing football 27
Station 2: We aren't singing 28
Station 3: Are you talking to me now? . . . 29
Station 4: Hobbies 30
Station 5: My favourite hobby 31
Station 6: In the free time 32
Station 7: Sports 33
Station 8: My favourite sport 34

At school
Station 1: School things 35
Station 2: Lessons 36
Station 2: Memory® cards 37
Station 3: Our school 38
Station 4: In our classroom 39
Station 5: Where is what? 40
Station 6: Classroom discourse 41
Station 7: In the gym 42
Station 8: The new teacher 43

Time to party (going to-future)
Station 1: I am going to have a party 44
Station 2: I am not going to do all this . . . 45
Station 3: Are you going to help me? 46
Station 4: The shopping list 47
Station 5: Food and drinks 48
Station 6: An invitation snake 49
Station 7: My party 50
Station 8: The new party outfit 51

Numbers, time, through the year, money
Station 1: Numbers from 1 to 100 52
Station 1: Memory® cards 53
Station 2: Numbers from 100 to 1 000 . . . 54
Station 3: Ordinal numbers 55
Station 4: What's the time, please? 56
Station 4: Cards 57
Station 5: It's ten o'clock now 58
Station 6: My day – telling the time 59
Station 7: My week 60
Station 8: British money 61
Station 9: A month's quiz 62

Questions

Station 1:	Where is it?	63
Station 2:	What is it?	64
Station 3:	When is it?	65
Station 4:	Why do you ask me?	66
Station 5:	How are you?	67
Station 6:	Who is it?	68
Station 7:	Question words I	69
Station 7:	Memory® cards	70
Station 8:	Question words II	71
Station 9:	Personal questions	72

Mixed up grammar topics

Station 1:	Articles	73
Station 2:	The genitive	74
Station 3:	A telephone call	75
Station 4:	Personal pronouns I	76
Station 5:	Personal pronouns II	77
Station 6:	Colours I	78
Station 7:	Colours II	79
Station 8:	Body parts	80
Station 9:	Clothing	81
Station 9:	Domino cards	82
Station 10:	Asking the way	83

Solutions 84

Vorwort

Bei den vorliegenden Stationsarbeiten handelt es sich um eine Arbeitsform, bei der unterschiedliche Lernvoraussetzungen, unterschiedliche Zugänge und Betrachtungsweisen und unterschiedliche Lern- und Arbeitstempi der Schüler[1] Berücksichtigung finden. Die Grundidee ist, den Schülern einzelne Arbeitsstationen anzubieten, an denen sie gleichzeitig selbstständig arbeiten können. Die Reihenfolge des Bearbeitens der Einzelstationen ist dabei ebenso frei wählbar wie das Arbeitstempo.

Als dominierende Unterrichtsprinzipien sind bei allen Stationen die Schüler- und Handlungsorientierung aufzuführen. Schülerorientierung meint, dass der Lehrer in den Hintergrund tritt und nicht mehr im Mittelpunkt der Interaktion steht. Er wird zum Beobachter, Berater und Moderator. Seine Aufgabe ist nicht das Strukturieren und Darbieten des Lerngegenstandes in kleinsten Schritten, sondern durch die vorbereiteten Stationen eine Lernatmosphäre zu schaffen, in der Schüler sich Unterrichtsinhalte eigenständig erarbeiten bzw. Lerninhalte festigen und vertiefen können.

Handlungsorientierung meint, dass das angebotene Material und die Arbeitsaufträge für sich selbst sprechen. Der Unterrichtsgegenstand und die zu gewinnenden Erkenntnisse werden nicht durch den Lehrer dargeboten, sondern durch die Auseinandersetzung mit dem Material und die eigene Tätigkeit gewonnen und begriffen.

Ziel der Veröffentlichung ist, wie bereits oben angesprochen, das Anknüpfen an unterschiedliche Lernvoraussetzungen der Schüler. Jeder Einzelne erhält seinen eigenen Zugang zum inhaltlichen Lernstoff. Die einzelnen Stationen ermöglichen das Lernen mit allen Sinnen bzw. den verschiedenen Eingangskanälen. Dabei werden sowohl visuelle (sehorientierte) als auch haptische (fühlorientierte) sowie intellektuelle Lerntypen angesprochen. An dieser Stelle werden auch gleichermaßen die Bruner'schen Repräsentationsebenen (enaktiv bzw. handelnd, ikonisch bzw. visuell und symbolisch) mit einbezogen. Aus Ergebnissen der Wissenschaft ist bekannt: Je mehr Eingangskanäle angesprochen werden, umso besser und langfristiger wird Wissen gespeichert und damit umso fester verankert. Das vorliegende Arbeitsheft unterstützt in diesem Zusammenhang das Erinnerungsvermögen, das nicht nur an Einzelheiten und Begriffe geknüpft ist, sondern häufig auch an die Lernsituation.

Folgende Inhalte des Englischunterrichts werden innerhalb der verschiedenen Stationen behandelt:

- at home (simple present)
- sports and hobbies (present progressive)
- at school
- time to party (going to-future)
- numbers, time, through the year, money
- questions
- mixed up grammar topics

---

[1] Wenn in diesem Arbeitsheft von Schüler gesprochen wird, ist auch immer die Schülerin gemeint. Ebenso verhält es sich mit Lehrer und Lehrerin etc.

Materialaufstellung und Hinweise zu den einzelnen Stationen

At home (simple present)

Die Seiten 10 bis 26 sind in entsprechender Anzahl zu vervielfältigen und den Schülern bereitzulegen. Als Möglichkeit zur Selbstkontrolle können Lösungsseiten erstellt werden. Manchmal sind offene Aufgaben mit individuellen Lösungen vorhanden, die im Plenum besprochen werden sollten. Spielkarten können laminiert werden.

Seite 10	Station 1	**My day:**	Ein Stift wird benötigt.
Seite 11	Station 2	**What we do on Saturdays:**	Ein Stift wird benötigt.
Seite 12	Station 3	**We don't and he doesn't:**	Ein Stift wird benötigt.
Seite 13	Station 4	**Do you like it?:**	Ein Stift und ein Heft werden benötigt.
Seite 14	Station 5	**Are you happy?:**	Ein Stift wird benötigt.
Seite 15	Station 6	**What I always do:**	Ein Stift wird benötigt.
Seite 16	Station 7	**Family members:**	Ein Klebestift, ein Stift, ein Heft und eine Schere werden benötigt.
Seite 17	Station 8	**About my family:**	Ein Stift und ein Heft werden benötigt.
Seite 18–19	Station 9	**Relationships:**	Ein Klebestift, ein Stift und eine Schere werden benötigt.
Seite 20	Station 10	**I have got a nice room:**	Ein Stift wird benötigt.
Seite 21	Station 11	**She hasn't got a sister:**	Ein Stift und ein Heft werden benötigt.
Seite 22	Station 12	**Rooms:**	Ein Klebestift, ein Stift, ein Heft und eine Schere werden benötigt.
Seite 23–24	Station 13	**Animals:**	Eine Schere und ein Stift werden benötigt.
Seite 25–26	Station 14	**Pets:**	Ein Klebestift, ein Stift und eine Schere werden benötigt.

Sports and hobbies (present progressive)

Die Seiten 27 bis 34 sind in entsprechender Anzahl zu vervielfältigen und den Schülern bereitzulegen. Als Möglichkeit zur Selbstkontrolle können Lösungsseiten erstellt werden. Manchmal sind offene Aufgaben mit individuellen Lösungen vorhanden, die im Plenum besprochen werden sollten. Spielkarten können laminiert werden.

Seite 27	Station 1	**I am playing football:**	Ein Stift und ein Heft werden benötigt.
Seite 28	Station 2	**We aren't singing:**	Ein Stift wird benötigt.
Seite 29	Station 3	**Are you talking to me now?:**	Ein Stift und ein Heft werden benötigt.
Seite 30	Station 4	**Hobbies:**	Ein Stift wird benötigt.
Seite 31	Station 5	**My favourite hobby:**	Ein Stift und ein Heft werden benötigt.
Seite 32	Station 6	**In the free time:**	Ein Stift, ein Heft und ein Lösungsblatt werden benötigt.
Seite 33	Station 7	**Sports:**	Ein Stift und ein Heft werden benötigt.
Seite 34	Station 8	**My favourite sport:**	Ein Stift und ein Heft werden benötigt.

At school

Die Seiten 35 bis 43 sind in entsprechender Anzahl zu vervielfältigen und den Schülern bereitzulegen. Als Möglichkeit zur Selbstkontrolle können Lösungsseiten erstellt werden. Manchmal sind offene Aufgaben mit individuellen Lösungen vorhanden, die im Plenum besprochen werden sollten. Spielkarten können laminiert werden.

Seite 35	Station 1	**School things:** Ein Stift wird benötigt.
Seite 36–37	Station 2	**Lessons:** Ein Stift und eine Schere werden benötigt.
Seite 38	Station 3	**Our school:** Ein Stift und ein Blatt weißes Papier werden benötigt.
Seite 39	Station 4	**In our classroom:** Ein Stift und ein Lösungsblatt werden benötigt.
Seite 40	Station 5	**Where is what?:** Ein Stift wird benötigt.
Seite 41	Station 6	**Classroom discourse:** Ein Stift und ein Vokabelheft werden benötigt.
Seite 42	Station 7	**In the gym:** Ein Stift und eine Schere werden benötigt.
Seite 43	Station 8	**The new teacher:** Ein Stift und ein Heft werden benötigt.

Time to party (going to-future)

Die Seiten 44 bis 51 sind in entsprechender Anzahl zu vervielfältigen und den Schülern bereitzulegen. Als Möglichkeit zur Selbstkontrolle können Lösungsseiten erstellt werden. Manchmal sind offene Aufgaben mit individuellen Lösungen vorhanden, die im Plenum besprochen werden sollten. Spielkarten können laminiert werden.

Seite 44	Station 1	**I am going to have a party:** Ein Stift wird benötigt.
Seite 45	Station 2	**I am not going to do all this:** Ein Stift und ein Heft werden benötigt.
Seite 46	Station 3	**Are you going to help me?:** Ein Stift wird benötigt.
Seite 47	Station 4	**The shopping list:** Ein Stift wird benötigt.
Seite 48	Station 5	**Food and drinks:** Ein Stift und ein Heft werden benötigt.
Seite 49	Station 6	**An invitation snake:** Ein Stift und ein Heft werden benötigt.
Seite 50	Station 7	**My party:** Ein Stift wird benötigt.
Seite 51	Station 8	**The new party outfit**: Ein Stift und ein Heft werden benötigt.

Numbers, time, through the year, money

Die Seiten 52 bis 62 sind in entsprechender Anzahl zu vervielfältigen und den Schülern bereitzulegen. Als Möglichkeit zur Selbstkontrolle können Lösungsseiten erstellt werden. Manchmal sind offene Aufgaben mit individuellen Lösungen vorhanden, die im Plenum besprochen werden sollten. Spielkarten können laminiert werden.

Seite 52–53	Station 1	**Numbers from 1 to 100:** Ein Stift und eine Schere werden benötigt.
Seite 54	Station 2	**Numbers from 100 to 1 000:** Ein Stift und das Englischbuch werden benötigt.
Seite 55	Station 3	**Ordinal numbers:** Ein Stift wird benötigt.
Seite 56–57	Station 4	**What's the time, please?:** Ein Stift, eine Schere, ein Klebestift, ein roter und ein blauer Filzstift werden benötigt.
Seite 58	Station 5	**It's ten o'clock now:** Eine Uhr mit verstellbaren Zeigern / eine Armbanduhr und ein Stift werden benötigt.
Seite 59	Station 6	**My day – telling the time:** Ein Stift und ein Heft werden benötigt.
Seite 60	Station 7	**My week:** Ein Stift und ein Heft werden benötigt.
Seite 61	Station 8	**British money:** Ein Stift wird benötigt.
Seite 62	Station 9	**A month's quiz:** Ein Stift wird benötigt.

Questions

Die Seiten 63 bis 72 sind in entsprechender Anzahl zu vervielfältigen und den Schülern bereitzulegen. Als Möglichkeit zur Selbstkontrolle können Lösungsseiten erstellt werden. Manchmal sind offene Aufgaben mit individuellen Lösungen vorhanden, die im Plenum besprochen werden sollten. Spielkarten können laminiert werden.

Seite 63	Station 1	**Where is it?:** Ein Stift wird benötigt.
Seite 64	Station 2	**What is it?:** Ein Stift und ein Vokabelheft werden benötigt.
Seite 65	Station 3	**When is it?:** Ein Stift und ein Heft werden benötigt.
Seite 66	Station 4	**Why do you ask me?:** Ein Stift wird benötigt.
Seite 67	Station 5	**How are you?:** Ein Stift wird benötigt.
Seite 68	Station 6	**Who is it?:** Ein Stift wird benötigt.
Seite 69–70	Station 7	**Question words I:** Ein Stift und eine Schere werden benötigt.
Seite 71	Station 8	**Question words II:** Ein Stift wird benötigt.
Seite 72	Station 9	**Personal questions:** Ein Stift wird benötigt.

Mixed up grammar topics

Die Seiten 73 bis 83 sind in entsprechender Anzahl zu vervielfältigen und den Schülern bereitzulegen. Als Möglichkeit zur Selbstkontrolle können Lösungsseiten erstellt werden. Manchmal sind offene Aufgaben mit individuellen Lösungen vorhanden, die im Plenum besprochen werden sollten. Spielkarten können laminiert werden.

Seite 73	Station 1	**Articles:** Ein Stift wird benötigt.
Seite 74	Station 2	**The genitive:** Ein Stift wird benötigt.
Seite 75	Station 3	**A telephone call:** Ein Stift und ein Heft werden benötigt.
Seite 76	Station 4	**Personal pronouns I:** Ein Stift, ein Heft und eine Schere werden benötigt.
Seite 77	Station 5	**Personal pronouns II:** Ein Stift wird benötigt.
Seite 78	Station 6	**Colours I:** Ein Stift wird benötigt.
Seite 79	Station 7	**Colours II:** Es werden je fünf verschiedenfarbige Gegenstände in zwei Kisten (Farben der Gegenstände auf einem Lösungsblatt notieren) und ein Stift benötigt.
Seite 80	Station 8	**Body parts:** Ein Stift wird benötigt.
Seite 81–82	Station 9	**Clothing:** Ein Stift, eine Schere und ein Heft werden benötigt.
Seite 83	Station 10	**Asking the way**

Route card

for _____

Obligatory stations

Station number	done	checked
number _____		
number _____		
number _____		
number _____		
number _____		
number _____		
number _____		
number _____		
number _____		

Optional station

Station number	done	checked
number _____		
number _____		
number _____		
number _____		
number _____		

Station 1

My day

Name: _____

 task
Fill in the correct English verbs. Take care of he, she, it – with an "s" at the end!

I _____ (aufstehen) at six o'clock in the morning and _____ (gehen) to the bathroom. There I _____ (putzen) my teeth, _____ (waschen) my face and _____ (kämmen) my hair.

I _____ (verlassen) the house at ten to seven. At a quarter past seven, I _____ (ankommen) at school. From half past seven till quarter to eight, we _____ (haben) breakfast together. The first lesson _____ (anfangen) at eight o'clock. After the first lesson we _____ (haben) a small break of fifteen minutes. At half past nine, we _____ (haben) a big break of thirty minutes. At ten o'clock, the next lesson _____ (beginnen). At quarter to eleven, we _____ (müssen) clean our classroom. After that, we _____ (haben) time to _____ (ausruhen), to _____ (reden) or to _____ (spielen) table tennis. After lunch, we _____ (machen/tun) different kinds of projects. We can _____ (wählen) between the wood working project, the photo or painting project and some sports.

At two o'clock, we _____ (können) go home. Then I _____ (machen) my homework.

After homework, I _____ (treffen) my friends, _____ (spielen) outside or _____ (schauen) TV. We _____ (essen) at eight o'clock when dad _____ (kommen) home. I _____ (gehen) to bed at nine o'clock in the evening.

---

brush   leave   have   start   talk   go   go   wash

do   comb   relax   begin   wake up   watch   arrive

do   play   meet   must   have   play   choose

have   can   eat   come   have

Station 2

What we do on Saturdays

Name:

 task 1

Write down what you normally do on Saturdays. Use the following verbs:

| eat | visit | help | read | go | get up | do | play | meet | sleep | watch | make |

1. _____
2. _____
3. _____
4. _____
5. _____
6. _____
7. _____
8. _____
9. _____
10. _____
11. _____
12. _____

 task 2

Write down what Peter and Sue do on Saturdays. Attention: he, she, it – "s".

do homework (Sue) _____

eat hamburgers (Peter) _____

get up at ten o'clock (Peter) _____

watch TV (Sue) _____

make breakfast (Sue) _____

go to bed late (Peter) _____

meet friends (Sue) _____

Station 3

We don't and he doesn't

Name:

At home (simple present)

task 1
Connect a small and a big box and write down the correct sentences.

Sarah		doesn't like its food today.
Tom		doesn't like homework.
The Millers		don't like their new English teacher.
Branda and Carol		doesn't write into her diary today.
Our cat		doesn't play with his friends in the garden.
My brother		don't watch TV very often.

1. _____
2. _____
3. _____
4. _____
5. _____
6. _____

task 2
Tick the right negation of the following sentences:

1. I like table tennis.
   - ☐ I don't like table tennis.
   - ☐ I not like table tennis.
   - ☐ I doesn't like table tennis.

2. Sarah plays tennis.
   - ☐ Sarah don't play tennis.
   - ☐ Sarah not plays tennis.
   - ☐ Sarah doesn't play tennis.

3. Peter and Tom like football.
   - ☐ Peter and Tom doesn't like football.
   - ☐ Peter and Tom don't like football.
   - ☐ Peter and Tom not like football.

Station 4

Do you like it?

Name:

 task 1

Find the correct short answers for the questions. Then copy the questions and answers into your exercise book.

Do you like shirts?	Yes, he does.
Does he live in London?	Yes, we do.
Do I play tennis well?	No, she doesn't.
Do the Millers like football?	Yes, I do.
Do we speak English well?	Yes, they do.
Does Sally play the piano?	No, you don't.

 task 2

Write down the correct questions to the following sentences:

1. Yes, she does her homework every day.

   _____

2. No, they don't like swimming.

   _____

3. Yes, he likes his computer game.

   _____

4. No, we don't eat hamburgers every day.

   _____

5. Yes, my mum helps me with my homework.

   _____

Station 5

At home (simple present)

Are you happy?

Name: _____

 task 1

Ask your partner the following questions and tick his/her answers in the chart. He/she must give you short answers.

Questions	Yes, I am / you are / he is / she is / it is / we are / you are / they are	No, I'm not / you aren't / he isn't / she isn't / it isn't / we aren't / you aren't / they aren't
Are you twelve?		
Are you from Berlin?		
Is your exercise book yellow?		
Is your best friend nice?		
Is your father a teacher?		
Is your mum beautiful?		
Is your exercise book on the table?		
Are you good in English?		
Are you new in this class?		
Are your pencils in your pencil case?		
Are your teachers nice?		
Are you happy today?		

task 2

Write down the correct questions to the following answers:

1. Yes, he is in my class. _____
2. No, they aren't happy today. _____
3. Yes, you are my best friend. _____
4. No, my parents aren't at work today. _____

Station 6

What I always do

Name: _____

task 1

Find the right signal words for the simple present and fill them in.

	simple present		

ALWAYS   SOMETIMES   AT THE MOMENT   USUALLY
NEVER   RIGHT NOW   JUST   TODAY   EVERY WEEK
NORMALLY   NOW   OFTEN   LOOK   THIS WEEK

task 2

Write down eight sentences and say what you usually, often, never, etc. do.

1. _____
2. _____
3. _____
4. _____
5. _____
6. _____
7. _____
8. _____

task 3

Read the sentences to your partner and listen to his/her sentences. Write down three things your partner usually, always, often, etc. does!

1. _____
2. _____
3. _____

Station 7

Family members

Name:

task 1

Cut out the cards below. Then find the cards that belong together and stick them into your exercise book.

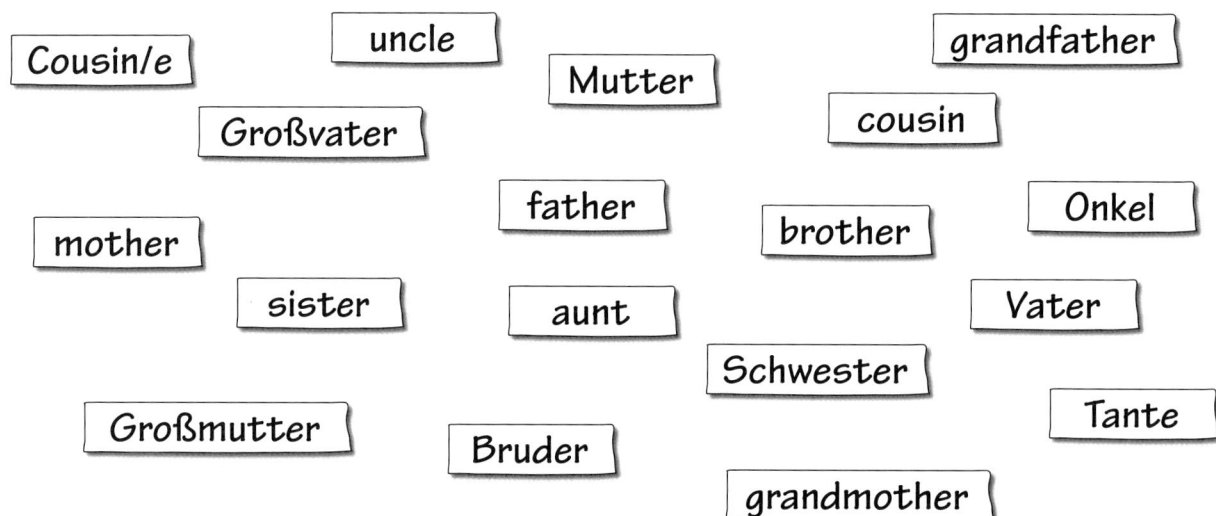

task 2

Fill in the missing English words:

1. Vater _ _ _ _ _ _
2. Großmutter _ _ _ _ _ _ _ _ _ _ _
3. Tante _ _ _ _
4. Schwester _ _ _ _ _ _
5. Cousine _ _ _ _ _ _
6. Großvater _ _ _ _ _ _ _ _ _ _ _

 or
task 3

Choose one family word and write down a line for every letter of your word. Let your partner(s) guess the correct word by telling the letters, that he/she thinks are in the word. For every right letter and the right solution your partner gets one point.

Example: Your word: _ _ _ _ _ _ (mother)

Your partner says: m, t, u, d, r, h and then knows the word.

Your partner has got five points: four points for the correct letters and one point for the correct word.

Station 8

About my family

Name: _____

 task 1

Write a short text about your family into your exercise book. You can use the sentences below.

My name is …	I am … years old.
I am from …	We have got a house/flat.
My parents aren't together. They are divorced.	
My father has got a new wife.	
My mother has got a new husband.	
My parents are … (nice, friendly, super, funny, …)	
My mother's name is …	She is … years old.
My father's name is …	He is … years old.
I have got … brother(s) and … sister(s).	I haven't got brothers or sisters.
My sister's name is …	She is … years old.
My brother's name is …	He is … years old.
My grandparents/grandma/grandpa is/are dead.	
I have got two grandmothers.	
My grandmothers' names are …	
My mother's mother is grandma …	Grandma … is … years old.
My father's mother is grandma …	Grandma … is … years old.
I have got two grandfathers.	
My grandfathers' names are …	
My mother's father is grandpa …	Grandpa … is … years old.
My father's father is grandpa …	Grandpa … is … years old.
My aunt's name is …	She is … years old.
She is my father's/mother's sister.	
My uncle's name is …	He is … years old.
He is my father's/mother's brother.	
I have … cousin(s).	
His/Her/Their name(s) is/are …	He/She/They is/are … years old.
I have got a pet.	I haven't got a pet.
It is a …	It's name is …
It's … years old.	

At home (simple present)

 task 2

Read your text to a partner and listen to his/her text.

Station 9

Relationships

Name:

task 1
Cut out the cards and stick the English solutions to the reverse side of the German sentences. Show the cards to your partner. He/she must translate the sentences for you. Correct his/her sentences with the help of the reverse of your card.

task 2
Look at the pictures of Sarah's family and write sentences about the family members. Start with: This is …/These are …

Station 9

Cards

Name:

At home (simple present)

Sarah hat einen Bruder. Sein Name ist Bill.	Sarah has got a brother. His name is Bill.
Mary und Tom mögen ihre Eltern.	Mary and Tom like/love their parents.
Peter kennt unsere Familie.	Peter knows our family.
Ich spiele immer mit meiner kleinen Schwester.	I always play with my little sister.
Meine Eltern kennen deine Eltern.	My parents know your parents.
Das ist unser Hund Sally.	This is our dog Sally.
Das ist meine Schwester. Ihr Name ist Sarah.	This is my sister. Her name is Sarah.
Gib mir das Bild, bitte!	Give me the picture/photo, please!
Seine Eltern sind in unserem Garten.	His parents are in our garden.

Station 10

Name:

I have got a nice room

task 1

Write down what you have got in your room. Mention (nennen) five things and their colours.

1. In my room, I have got _____
2. _____
3. _____
4. _____
5. _____

task 2

Look at the picture and write down what Peter has got in his room.

1. In his room, Peter has got _____
2. _____
3. _____
4. _____
5. _____
6. _____
7. _____
8. _____
9. _____

At home (simple present)

Station 11

She hasn't got a sister

Name:

task 1

1. Ask one pupil in your class about his/her family. Tick his/her answers in the chart below.

Question	Yes, he/she has	No, he/she hasn't	Name of the pupil
Have you got a garden?			
Have you got a brother?			
Have you got a hamster?			
Have you got a dog?			
Have you got a sister?			
Have you got a house?			

2. Write down what your classmate has and hasn't got.
   Example: Mike has got a sister. Mike hasn't got a brother. Etc.

1. _____
2. _____
3. _____
4. _____
5. _____
6. _____

task 2

Find the correct pairs and write the complete dialogues into your exercise book.

Yes, she has.	Yes, I have.	Have you got a cat?
No, they haven't.	Have we got our homework?
Yes, we have.	No, he hasn't.	Have they got a dog?
Has he got a younger brother?	Has she got my book?

At home (simple present)

Station 12

Rooms

Name:

task 1

Cut out the cards and stick the correct solution to the reverse side of the description. Partner 1 reads the text on the card to his/her partner. Partner 2 must guess which room in the house Partner 1 is talking about. Then Partner 2 reads out the next card. Correct your partner, if he/she is wrong.

This room normally is very small. You will find a mirror and a washbasin. There are tiles on the walls. Guests go there to wash hands or to use the toilet.	toilet
In this room you cook or bake. Sometimes people eat in this room, too. You will find a cooker, a washbasin, and sometimes a table with chairs. Some people have got a dishwasher in this room.	kitchen
In this room the family sits together in the evening and watches TV or plays games. You often find a TV, couches, and a small table in this room. It's very often the biggest room in a house or flat.	living room
In this room you find your bed, your shelves, and your wardrobe. Here you have got your toys, and everything you need.	children's room
In this room your mum or dad works. Very often there is a telephone, a computer, and some shelves in it.	study room/office room
In this room you normally find a washbasin, the bath tub, a shower, and a mirror. Everybody uses this room in the morning and in the evening.	bathroom

task 2

Take your exercise book and make a mind map of your house. Fill in the words for the rooms and the furniture inside.

Station 13

Animals

Name: _____

 task 1

Cut out the domino cards. Watch out: Don't separate the picture from the word, only separate the domino cards. Then play domino and find the right word for each animal.

 task 2

Write down one sentence for each animal in which you describe it. Don't mention (nennen) the animal's name.

1. This animal _____

2. _____

3. _____

4. _____

5. _____

6. _____

7. _____

8. _____

9. _____

10. _____

 task 3

Read out three of your sentences to a partner and let him/her guess which animals you mean. Then listen to his/her sentences and guess his/her animals.

Station 13

Domino cards

Name:

At home (simple present)

bird	*(crocodile)*
crocodile	*(kangaroo)*
kangaroo	*(duck)*
duck	*(snake)*
snake	*(polar bear)*
polar bear	*(dog)*
dog	*(rabbit)*
rabbit	*(cat)*
cat	*(elephant)*
elephant	*(bird)*

Station 14

Pets

Name:

At home (simple present)

task 1
Cut out the cards and stick the correct word to the reverse side of the picture. Show the pictures to your partner and let him/her guess the name of the pets. He/she has to say: In the picture, I see a … Correct him/her by reading out the reverse side of the card.

task 2
Which pet is it? Read the following sentences and write down the correct name of the pet.

1. It's the man's best friend. You must go for a walk with this pet every day.

2. It's smaller than a dog and it loves mice.

3. This pet is very small and it lives in a cage. It's yellow and brown and it doesn't sleep at night.

4. This pet lives in a cage. It can sing and sometimes it speaks some words.

5. This pet lives in an aquarium. It swims around and can have many colours.

6. It's a very small pet and many women scream when they see one.

7. This pet loves carrots and it moves by hopping.

Station 14

Cards

Name:

At home (simple present)

	hamster		budgie
	goldfish		mouse
	rabbit		cat
	dog		guinea pig
	parrot		tortoise
	snake		frog

Station 1

Name:

I am playing football

 task 1

Connect the boxes and write sentences about what you are doing into your exercise book.

sitting		in the garden
playing		on the sofa
helping my mum		with the dog
singing		for a vocabulary test
going for a walk		basketball with my friend
learning		a song

Sports and hobbies (present progressive)

 task 2

Fill the gaps with the right present progressive form.

1. Look, Peter _____ (play) in the garden with our dog.

2. The dog _____ (run) after the ball.

3. Now, Peter _____ (come) into the house.

   He _____ (go) into the kitchen.

4. Mum and dad _____ (sit) in the living room.

   They _____ (watch) TV.

5. At the moment, Peter's sister _____ (learn) for an English test on Monday.

6. Now, Peter _____ (leave) again.

   He _____ (take) his bike to ride to the football field.

7. The boys _____ (play) football now.

Station 2

We aren't singing

Name:

task 1
Look at the pictures and tell your partner what the kids aren't doing at the moment.
Start like this: At the moment, the boy ...

1.
2.
3.
4.
5.

task 2
Read the following sentences and write down in English what the people aren't doing now.

1. Peter spielt gerade nicht mit seiner Schwester.

2. Mama und Papa schauen gerade nicht fern.

3. Sarah lernt gerade nicht für ihren Englischtest.

4. Tom spielt gerade nicht mit seinen Freunden Fußball.

5. Die Müllers treffen gerade nicht ihre Freunde.

6. Donna und Mary gehen gerade nicht spazieren.

Station 3

Are you talking to me now?

Name:

task 1
Write down the correct questions to the following answers.

1. No, he isn't playing football now.

   Is he _____

2. No, she isn't going for a walk with the dog.

   _____

3. Yes, the trainers are talking to their teams now.

   _____

4. Yes, the kids are playing the piano at the moment.

   _____

5. No, we aren't playing basketball right now.

   _____

6. Yes, I am swimming at the moment.

   _____

task 2
Note questions for your partner with the help of the words below. Use the present progressive. Read the questions to your partner and note his answers in your exercise book. Now listen to your partner's questions and answer them orally.

1. Are you _____

2. _____

3. _____

4. _____

learn English now   play tennis at the moment

dream of a good mark in Englisch   work with a partner now

look out of the window at the moment   meet friends now

do homework right now   drink tea at the moment

Sports and hobbies (present progressive)

Station 4

Hobbies

Name:

Sports and hobbies (present progressive)

 task

Ask your partner about his hobbies and tick his hobbies in the chart below. Fill in the chart for yourself. Choose nine hobbies and write sentences about yourself, your partner, Sarah or Tommy. Use the present progressive.

	you	your partner	Sarah	Tommy
listen to music			X	
read books			X	
play basketball				X
cook			X	
fish				X
sing				X
dive				
write poems			X	
go to the theatre				
play games				X
write emails			X	X

1. Sarah is listening to music.
2. _____
3. _____
4. _____
5. _____
6. _____
7. _____
8. _____
9. _____

Station 5

My favourite hobby

Name:

 task 1

Find the English translation for the German hobbies below in the puzzle. Write the English word down.

A	G	H	B	I	K	I	N	G	F	D	R	P
N	H	G	F	T	R	D	U	H	N	G	R	L
C	J	G	Z	T	R	J	S	I	N	H	F	A
O	K	U	L	H	Z	J	H	S	H	K	J	Y
O	R	E	A	D	I	N	G	J	O	H	O	I
K	H	D	S	J	V	S	J	F	U	N	G	N
I	W	A	T	C	H	I	N	G	T	V	G	G
N	J	N	S	E	R	N	E	R	U	R	I	S
G	P	C	Q	S	C	G	D	F	N	A	N	G
G	H	I	S	K	I	I	N	G	R	A	G	E
J	K	N	Y	B	F	N	F	V	M	L	W	W
K	H	G	L	A	M	G	H	T	Z	F	D	D

1. Fahrrad fahren _____
2. fernsehen _____
3. lesen _____
4. kochen _____
5. joggen _____
6. spielen _____
7. tanzen _____
8. Ski fahren _____
9. singen _____

 task 2

Write a short text about your favourite hobby into your exercise book. Your text should not be longer than five sentences. Read your text to a partner and listen to his text.

Station 6

In the free time

Name:

Sports and hobbies (present progressive)

 task

1. Partner 1 chooses five pictures and tells his/her partner what the kids are doing in their free time. Partner 2 listens to his/her partner and corrects the sentences with the help of the solution sheet. Change roles afterwards.

Mary

Tom and Judy

Jonny

the class

Julia

Anna

Carol and Jim

Sue and Carla

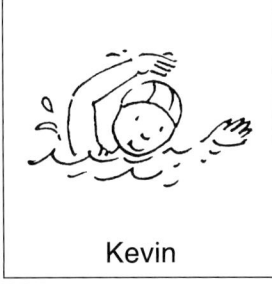
Kevin

David

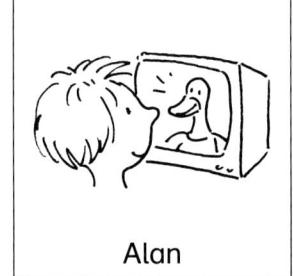
Alan

Frank and Tony

Marilyn

Kate

Lisa

Toby

2. Write five sentences about what the kids are doing into your exercise book and compare then with your partner.

32

Station 7

Sports

Name: _____

 task 1

Copy the chart below into your exercise book. Read the words and fill them correctly into your chart.

football   bat   basketball   swimmer   skates   football   racket
skis   basket   catch   skating   ball   athlete   skiing
badminton player   shoot   basketball player   boxer   swim   cyclist
football player   skater   surfer   tennis player   ring   volleyball player
win   coach   court   gym   stadium   net   athletics   skate
badminton   ping-pong   riding   surfing   swimming   tennis   volleyball
windsurfing   beat   cycle   hit   kick   cycling   lose   trainer
practice   ride   throw   play   basketball

Sports and hobbies (present progressive)

	sports	verbs	places	people	equipment
1					
2					
...					

task 2

What's the name of the sport?

1. You play _____ in a team of eleven men or women and you need a ball.

2. You play _____ against another player on a table. You need a small white ball.

3. You play _____ in a team of five players and you need a ball. You must throw the ball into a basket.

4. When you do _____, you are in the water and can move in it really quickly.

5. You play _____ against one other player or you play in a team of two against another team. You need a racket and a small yellow ball.

Station 8

My favourite sport

Name: _____

task 1
Write down the sports the kids are doing.

1. Sam _____ (spielen) _____ (Fußball) at the moment.

2. Mary _____ (reiten) _____ (ihr Pferd) now.

3. Thomas and Kevin _____ (spielen) _____ (Tennis) in the garden right now.

4. Look, Jenny _____ (schwimmen).

5. At the moment, the two teams _____ (spielen) _____ (Tischtennis).

task 2
At the moment, the kids are doing their favourite sports. Write down what they are doing.

1. John _____

2. Tom _____

3. Carol and her sister _____

4. Sam and Perry _____

5. The girls in my class _____

task 3
Write a short text about your favourite sport into your exercise book. Imagine, you are doing it right now and you are telling somebody what you are doing.

Sports and hobbies (present progressive)

Station 1

School things

Name:

task 1
Find the school things below in the word puzzle.

A	G	F	E	L	T	T	I	P	H	U	P	L
B	P	E	N	B	H	F	D	B	H	T	E	R
S	C	H	O	O	L	B	A	G	K	S	N	U
P	K	N	P	E	N	C	I	L	K	H	C	B
H	T	G	V	J	R	U	B	F	E	A	I	B
N	R	J	G	F	J	N	V	I	H	R	L	E
G	U	G	K	O	J	G	R	R	N	P	C	R
F	L	L	H	L	N	L	F	O	M	E	A	D
V	E	R	E	D	Z	U	S	H	L	N	S	Z
S	R	R	G	E	N	E	T	R	H	E	E	I
B	O	O	K	R	D	K	J	R	U	R	J	I
E	X	E	R	C	I	S	E	B	O	O	K	L

book   ruler   sharpener   schoolbag   rubber   felt tip   pencil
pencil case   pen   exercise book   folder   glue

task 2
Translate the English words into German.

1. book _____
2. rubber _____
3. pen _____
4. ruler _____
5. sharpener _____
6. schoolbag _____
7. pencil case _____
8. exercise book _____
9. folder _____
10. glue _____
11. felt tip _____
12. pencil _____

At school

Station 2

Lessons

Name:

task 1
Cut out the cards and play memory® with a partner. Find the lessons that go together. The one who finds most of the pairs is the winner.

task 2
Write your own lesson plan.

Monday	Tuesday	Wednesday	Thursday	Friday

Station 2

Memory® cards

Name: _____

English	Englisch	German	Deutsch
PE	Sport	Art	Kunst
Music	Musik	Geography	Erdkunde
French	Französisch	Maths	Mathematik
Drama group	Theatergruppe	RE	Religion
Biology	Biologie	History	Geschichte
Science	Naturwissenschaften	Break	Pause

At school

Station 3

Our school

Name:

 task

Partner 1 reads the text to partner 2. Read very slowly. Partner 2 must draw a picture of the story. Now change roles so that partner 2 reads out the text and partner 2 draws a picture to it. Compare your pictures and reread the text to see if everything is correct.

In the middle of the picture there is a school building.
On the right-hand-side there is a big bus.
Three kids are sitting inside.
On the left-hand-side there is a big green tree.
Seven apples hang on it.
In front of the school there is a street.
Behind the school there are three hills and in front of the hills there is another street.
On top of the hills there are three cars.
The sun is shining.
There are also five clouds.
On the left-hand-side of the school there is also a fence.
Behind the fence there is a teacher.
Next to the teacher there is a bin.
In the sky there are two birds.

Station 4

In our classroom

Name: _____

 task 1

Look at the chart below. Tell your partner what is in the classroom and what isn't there. Your partner will check your sentences with the solution sheet. Then listen to your partner and check his sentences. Start like this: There is/are … There isn't/aren't …

Things in the classroom	yes	no
1. board	✗	
2. tables	✗	
3. chairs	✗	
4. playstation		✗
5. windows	✗	
6. desk	✗	
7. car		✗
8. sofas		✗
9. toilet		✗

task 2

Write down the sentences. Compare them with your partner and correct your partner's sentences with the help of the solution sheet, if necessary.

1. _____
2. _____
3. _____
4. _____
5. _____
6. _____
7. _____
8. _____
9. _____

Station 5

Where is what?

Name:

 task 1

Fill in the right prepositions.

1. My book is _____ (unter) the table.
2. The chair is _____ (hinter) the desk.
3. The pencil is _____ (in) my pencil case.
4. The board is _____ (neben) the door.
5. The pictures are _____ (an) the wall.
6. Our exercise books are _____ (auf) the table.
7. The girls are sitting _____ (hinter) the boys in the classroom.

 task 2

Look at the pictures and say where the things and people are.

1.  _____

2.  _____

3.  _____

4.  _____

5.  _____

6.  _____

Station 6

Classroom discourse

Name:

task
Find the bubbles that fit together and write the sentences/questions into your vocabulary book.

- I'm sorry I'm late.
- Könnten Sie das bitte noch einmal sagen?
- Sorry, I don't understand this.
- Könnten sie das bitte an die Tafel schreiben?
- Was haben wir auf?
- What does … mean?
- What's … in German/in English?
- Entschuldigung, ich habe meine Hausaufgabe nicht gemacht.
- Could you help me, please?
- Was heißt … auf Deutsch/auf Englisch?
- Entschuldigung, ich verstehe das nicht.
- Could you write it on the board, please?
- Könnten Sie mir bitte helfen?
- Sorry, I haven't done my homework.
- What's the homework?
- Could you say it again, please?
- Entschuldigung, dass ich zu spät komme.
- Was bedeutet …?

At school

Station 7

In the gym

Name: _____

task 1

Fill in the right prepositions: in (2 x), on (2 x), next to, in front of, behind, under.

1. The ball is _____ my hand.
2. The players stand _____ the goal.
3. The teacher always stands _____ the line.
4. The school bags are _____ the changing stall (Umkleidekabine).
5. You can see our points _____ the chart.
6. The rackets are _____ the balls.
7. We sit _____ the floor and talk to each other.
8. My shoes are _____ the chair.

task 2

Cut out the cards. Then mix the cards and play memory®. The one with the most pairs in the end is the winner of this game.

gym	Turnhalle	basket	Korb
net	Netz	change	umziehen
goal	Tor	play	spielen
players	Spieler	win	gewinnen

Station 8

The new teacher

Name:

task 1

Mr. Miller, the director of the middle school, comes into the class to present the new German teacher. The class is very happy because they don't like their old German teacher. He always writes lots of tests.

Read the following dialogue.

Mr. Miller:	"Good morning, class."
Class:	"Good morning, Mr. Miller."
Mr. Miller:	"Look, this is Mr. Althaus. He is your new German teacher. Do you have any questions for him?
Sarah:	"Mr. Althaus, where are you from in Germany?"
Mr. Althaus:	"I am from Berlin."
Tom:	"And do you have a family?"
Mr. Althaus:	"Yes, I have got a wife and three children. A boy and two girls."
Mary:	"How old are your children?"
Mr. Althaus:	"The boy is ten years old and the girls are twelve."
Harry:	"Oh, so the girls are twins?"
Mr. Althaus:	"Yes, they are. Do you have twins in your class?"
Harry:	"No, we don't."
Peter:	"Mr. Althaus, why do you live in London now?"
Mr. Althaus:	"Because my wife has got a new job in London. And now, I have got a new job here, too. That's nice."
Sally:	"Well, when is our first German lesson with you?"
Mr. Althaus:	"Oh, the first German lesson is right now. Please take out your exercise books. We write a short German test."
Class:	"Oh no … He is like our old German teacher!"

task 2

Answer the questions below in your exercise book.

1. What's the name of the new German teacher?
2. Who asks him the first questions?
3. What does Mary want to know?
4. Does the teacher have children?
5. Why does the German teacher live in London now?
6. What is the first thing the class must do in their first lesson with the new German teacher?

Station 1

I am going to have a party

Name:

task 1

Fill in the correct form of the going-to-future.

1. Sarah and I _____ (have) a party tomorrow.

2. My best friend Sally _____ (come), too.

3. Peter _____ (help) me with the hamburgers.

4. Our parents _____ (prepare) the garage for the party.

5. On Saturday, my best friend Carol _____ (have) her birthday party.

6. I _____ (go) there at seven o'clock.

7. My brother Terry and his friend James _____ (come) with me.

8. On Sunday, we _____ (sleep) long, I think.

task 2

Write sentences about what the kids are going to prepare for the party.

1. – go

_____

2.  – buy

_____

3.  – make

_____

4.  – bring/garage

_____

5.  – prepare

_____

Station 2

I am not going to do all this

Name:

task 1

Sarah tells her sister what she is going to do on Saturday. Mary tells her that she isn't going to do all these things. Write down Mary's sentences.

- Dad and I are going to play the piano.
- I'm going to go swimming tomorrow morning.
- Peter and I are going to buy a present for grandma.
- I'm going to take the dog for a walk.
- I am going to read a good book in the afternoon.
- Mum and I are going to prepare the Christmas tree.

1. _____
2. _____
3. _____
4. _____
5. _____
6. _____

task 2

Ask three people in your classroom what they are NOT going to do today and write their answers into your exercise book.

Station 3

Are you going to help me?

Name:

task 1
The words of these sentences are mixed up. Bring them in the correct order.

1. you / going to / are / me / help / ?

2. is / going to / mother / your / everything / buy / the / party / for / ?

3. your / make / brother / going to / is / music / ?

4. Sarah / come / going to / too / is / , / ?

5. we / going to / are / games / play / funny / ?

6. dad / your / going to / help / you / the / hamburgers / with / is / ?

task 2
Tick the right questions for the following answers.

1. Yes, we are going to have fun.
   - ☐ Are you going to have fun?
   - ☐ Is she going to have fun?
   - ☐ Am I going to have fun?

2. No, she isn't going to eat salad.
   - ☐ Are they going to eat salad?
   - ☐ Is she going to eat salad?
   - ☐ Are you going to eat salad?

3. Yes, you are going to dance with me.
   - ☐ Is he going to dance with you?
   - ☐ Are you going to dance with me?
   - ☐ Am I going to dance with you?

4. No, they aren't going to sleep early.
   - ☐ Are they going to sleep early?
   - ☐ Is she going to sleep early?
   - ☐ Are you going to sleep early?

Station 4

The shopping list

Name:

 task 1

Read the dialogue in a group of three.

Perry: "Good morning Sarah, are you going to help me with the party this afternoon?"
Sarah: "Yes, I am going to go to the supermarket for you."
Perry: "Oh, that's nice. Is mum going to go with you?"
Mum: "No, I am going to prepare the drinks for tonight and dad is going to clean the garage for the party."
Perry: "Well, then I am going to go with Sarah. Are we going to meet some other friends there?"
Sarah: "Yes, I think Peter and Jim are going to come and help us. What are we going to buy?
Mum: "Well, I am going to make a salad and hamburgers so I need a lot of vegetables and bread, cheese and some meat."
Sarah: "So we are going to need a big basket!"
Perry: "Yes, I think so. Well, then we are going to take the bus at two o'clock, OK? Mum, are you going to write a list for us?"
Mum: "Yes, I am going to give it to you before you leave the house."
Sarah: "Perfect, then I am going to look for the CDs for tonight now."

 task 2

Answer the questions below.

1. Who is going to have a party tonight?

   _____

2. Is Sarah going to go to the supermarket alone?

   _____

3. Who is going to come to the supermarket, too?

   _____

4. What is Perry's mum going to prepare for the party?

   _____

5. When are the kids going to take the bus?

   _____

6. When is Perry's mum going to give the shopping list to the kids?

   _____

Time to party (going to-future)

Station 5

Food and drinks

Name:

task 1

You want to prepare hamburgers and a fruit salad for your party. Tick the things you need.

- ice-cubes ☐
- pepper ☐
- a sauce pan ☐
- a toaster ☐
- lettuce ☐
- tomatoes ☐
- cheese ☐
- a spoon ☐
- water ☐
- onions ☐
- oranges ☐
- meat ☐
- a knife ☐
- a bowl ☐
- pears ☐
- buns ☐
- butter ☐
- lemons ☐
- a plate ☐
- milk ☐
- a cup ☐
- kiwis ☐
- a fork ☐
- tea ☐
- bananas ☐
- apples ☐
- a steak ☐
- grapes ☐
- chips ☐
- melon ☐
- sugar ☐
- pineapple ☐

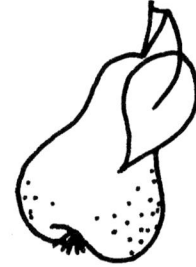

Time to party (going to-future)

task 2

1. Write a short recipe for a meal you like into your exercise book.
2. Give the recipe to a partner. He/She must translate it into German.
3. Translate your partner's recipe into German, too.
4. Compare your German translations with the original English recipe and correct it, if necessary.

Station 6

An invitation snake

Name: _____

 task
Write the invitation to Peter's party correctly into your exercise book.

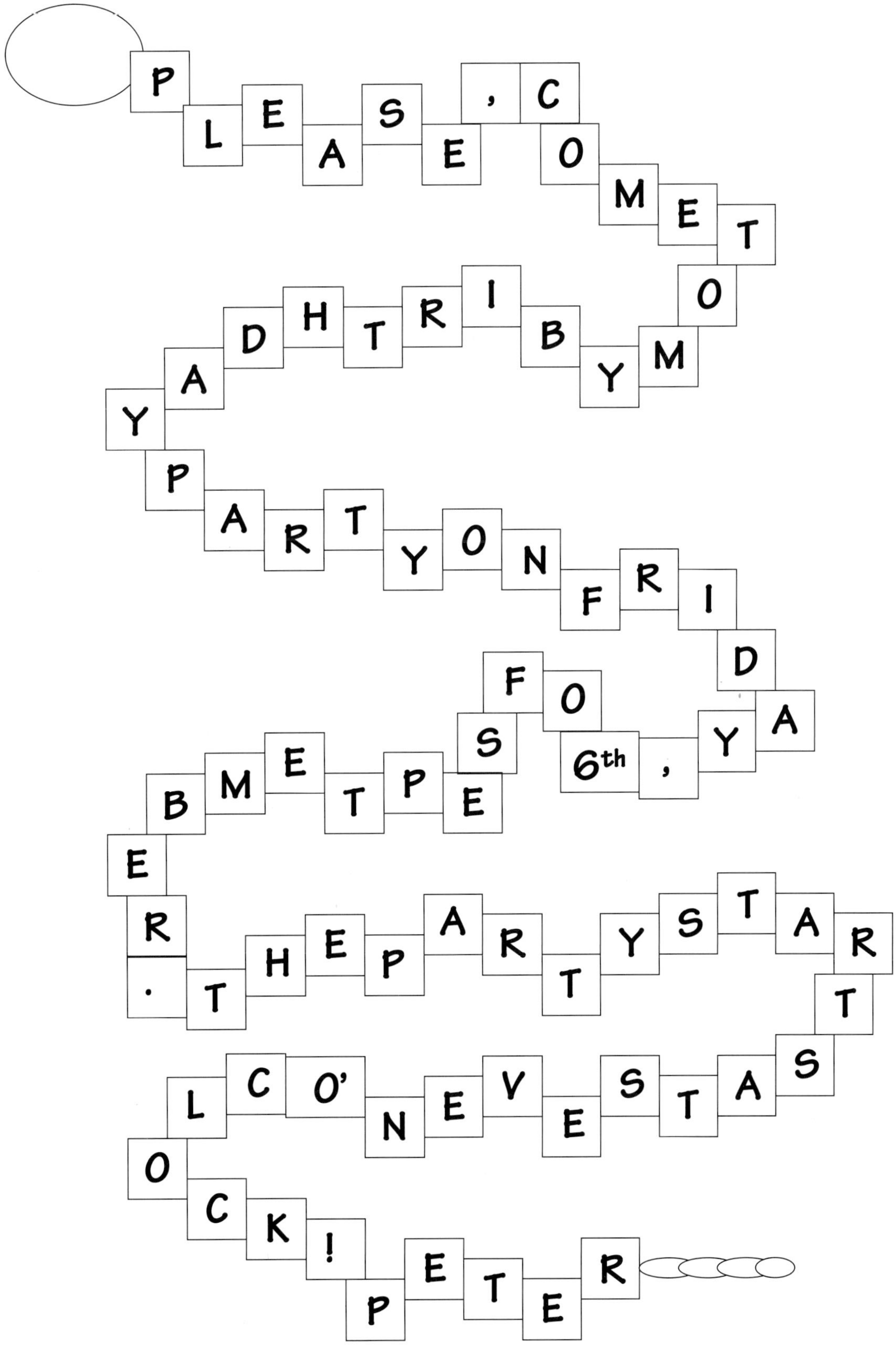

Please, come to my birthday party on Friday, 6th of September. The party starts at seven o'clock! Peter

Time to party (going to-future)

Station 7

My party

Name:

 task 1

Write down what you are going to do to prepare your birthday party.

1. buy hamburgers
2. bring tables and chairs into the garage
3. invite friends
4. buy new CDs
5. ask your parents for help
6. call some friends for help

1. _____
2. _____
3. _____
4. _____
5. _____
6. _____

 task 2

Write down a creative invitation card to your birthday party. Don't forget:

1. the headline (What kind of a party is it?)
2. when
3. where

_____
_____
_____
_____
_____
_____
_____

Station 8

The new party outfit

Name:

task 1
Translate the following shopping dialogue into English and write it into your exercise book.

Kunde:	„Guten Tag."
Verkäufer:	„Guten Tag. Kann ich Ihnen helfen?"
Kunde:	„Ja bitte. Ich mache eine Party am Samstag und brauche eine neue Hose."
Verkäufer:	„Bitte sehr. Größe acht."
Kunde:	„Vielen Dank. Ich probiere sie an."
Verkäufer:	„Passt sie? Gefällt Ihnen die Farbe?"
Kunde:	„Ja, sie passt, aber sie gefällt mir nicht in blau."
Verkäufer:	„Wie wäre es mit der weißen Hose?"
Kunde:	„Ja, die ist schön. Ich brauche auch noch ein T-Shirt."
Verkäufer:	„In welcher Größe und in welcher Farbe, bitte?"
Kunde:	„Größe S, bitte. Und ich hätte es gern in schwarz."
Verkäufer:	„Bitte sehr. Passt es?"
Kunde:	„Ja, danke. Wie viel kostet es?"
Verkäufer:	„Das T-Shirt kostet 20 Pfund. Es sieht gut aus. Möchten Sie die Sachen nehmen?"
Kunde:	„Ja, das möchte ich."
Verkäufer:	„Vielen Dank."
Kunde:	„Auf Wiedersehen."
Verkäufer:	„Auf Wiedersehen."

task 2
Compare your translation with your partner's translation before you check the solution. Correct your dialogues. Read the dialogue with your partner.

Time to party (going to-future)

Station 1

Numbers from 1 to 100

Name:

task 1

Write down the correct numbers in English.

3	_____	13	_____
21	_____	92	_____
39	_____	12	_____
17	_____	59	_____
11	_____	75	_____
44	_____	30	_____
53	_____	9	_____
68	_____	48	_____
70	_____	60	_____
82	_____	5	_____
99	_____	3	_____
100	_____	88	_____

task 2

Cut out the memory® cards before you start to play. Play the memory® game with a partner. The one who finds most of the pairs is the winner.

task 3

Take three number-cards from the memory® game and show them to your partner. He/she must write down the numbers in English. Control the numbers with the memory® cards.

1. _____
2. _____
3. _____

Station 1

Memory® cards

Name:

7	seven	9	nine
15	fifteen	12	twelve
21	twenty-one	45	forty-five
86	eighty-six	38	thirty-eight
91	ninety-one	66	sixty-six
100	one hundred	74	seventy-four

Station 2

Numbers from 100 to 1 000

Name:

 task 1

Connect the right numbers.

320	Five hundred nineteen
490	One hundred two
102	Six hundred seventy-seven
519	One thousand
677	Eight hundred ninety-one
723	Three hundred twenty
891	Four hundred ninety
999	Seven hundred twenty-three
1 000	Nine hundred ninety-nine

 task 2

1. Every one of you writes down five numbers between 100 and 1 000 in English words.

2. Read the numbers to your partner and let him/her note the number in digits (Ziffern).

3. Correct your partner's digits with the help of your written numbers and your English book (if necessary). The one with the most correct digits is the winner.

Station 3

Ordinal numbers

Name:

task 1

Fill in the chart.

	number	ordinal number	short form
1			
2		second	
3			
5	five		5th
8			
10			
21			
33			
40			
79			
100			

task 2

Write down the birthday dates of Sarah's family in English words.

1. Mum 3.12.: _____

2. Dad 21.5.: _____

3. Peter 1.1.: _____

4. Sarah 2.6.: _____

5. Grandma 31.8.: _____

6. Grandpa 5.7.: _____

Station 4

What's the time, please?

Name:

 task 1

Cut out the cards and stick the time-cards to the reverse of the cards with the correct sentences.

1. Take five cards. Show the cards to your partner and let him/her tell you the time. Correct the time by using the reverse side of your time-card, if necessary.

2. Take five new cards and write down the times of your partner's cards. Correct yourselves by using the reverse side of the cards.

 task 2

Fill in the time correctly. Use a red pen for the hours and a blue pen for the minutes.

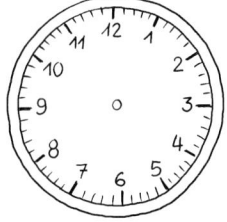   It's seven thirty.

   It's a quarter past nine.

   It's a quarter to ten.

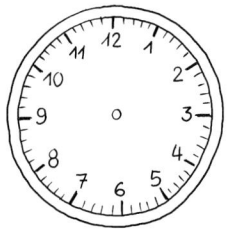   It's midnight.

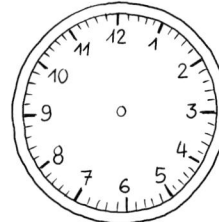   It's a quarter past one.

Station 4

Cards

Name: _____

4:15	It's a quarter past four.	20:30	It's half past eight.
13:45	It's a quarter to two.	3:15	It's a quarter past three.
19:50	It's ten (minutes) to eight.	21:30	It's half past nine.
2:00	It's two o'clock.	16:00	It's four o'clock.
17:20	It's twenty (minutes) past five.	8:56	It's four (minutes) to nine.
00:00	It's midnight./ It's twelve o'clock.	10:03	It's three (minutes) past ten.

Station 5

It's ten o'clock now

Name:

task 1

Check the time with your partner. Take a clock or watch and set a time you want to know. Only take full hours. Your partner tells you the time.
Start like this: It's ... o'clock now. Everyone sets the clock five times.

task 2

Write down the correct time in a full sentence.

03:45
04:30
07:05
09:00
12:45
18:15
07:50
01:00
14:40
17:10
15:06
02:47
01:30
15:30
08:09
16:45
19:03
22:00
00:00

Station 6

My day – telling the time

Name:

task 1
Look at the plan of Sarah's day and write down when she does what on Monday.

time	Monday
8:00	go to school
13:15	arrive at home
14:30	have lunch
16:00	do homework
17:45	watch TV
19:15	eat with the family
20:30	take a shower
21:00	go to bed

1. At eight o'clock, Sarah _____
2. _____
3. _____
4. _____
5. _____
6. _____
7. _____
8. _____

task 2
Write into your exercise book what you do on Monday. Don't forget to tell the time.

Station 7

My week

Name: _____

 task 1

Sarah calls her English pen friend and tells her what she does every day. Translate her German sentences into English.

1. Montags gehe ich immer schwimmen.
2. Dienstags und mittwochs habe ich Klavierstunden.
3. Donnerstags treffe ich meine Freunde nach der Schule.
4. Freitags mache ich für gewöhnlich all meine Hausaufgaben und gehe dann mit dem Hund spazieren.
5. Samstags schlafe ich lange. Nachmittags besuchen wir meine Großeltern.
6. Sonntags reite ich mein Pferd und manchmal treffe ich meine Freunde.

1. _____
2. _____
3. _____
4. _____
5. _____
6. _____

 task 2

Think about your week and write into your exercise book what you do every single day. Read your text to a partner and listen to her/his text.

Station 8

British money

Name:

 task
Write the correct prices into the chart below.

> one hundred pounds   thirteen pounds
> fifteen pence   three pounds thirty
> four pounds   one penny
> forty pence   eight pounds ninety
> one pound   six pounds forty-five
> forty-five pence   two pounds ninety
> two pounds forty   fifty-five pence

£ 1	
£ 13	
£ 4	
£ 8.90	
40p	
1p	
£ 6.45	
45p	
£ 2.90	
£ 100	
55p	
15p	
£ 2.40	
£ 3.30	

Station 9

A month's quiz

Name:

task 1
Find the correct months for the following descriptions and write new sentences.

1. These months have got 30 days.
2. These months have got 31 days.
3. This month has got 28 or 29 days.
4. These months are in summer.
5. These months are in winter.
6. These months are rather warm.
7. This month has got three letters.
8. These months have got a "y" in them.

November | March | October | May | January | September | August | June | July | December | April | February

1. April, _____
2. _____
3. _____
4. _____
5. _____
6. _____
7. _____
8. _____

task 2
Ask six pupils in your class about the month and the date of their birthday and write down sentences. Start with your own birthday:

1. My birthday is in _____
2. _____
3. _____
4. _____
5. _____
6. _____
7. _____

Station 1

Where is it?

Name:

task 1

Fill in the numbers of the correct questions to the following sentences.

1. It's under the table.
2. They are in the kitchen.
3. I think she is at school.
4. He is playing in the garden.
5. They are in your shelves.
6. She is in the kitchen and helps dad with the breakfast.

1. Where is your sister Sally?
2. Where is your hamster?
3. Where is Ben?
4. Where is mum at the moment?
5. Where are my books?
6. Where are all our plates and spoons?

task 2

Write down the correct questions with "where".

1. We do our homework in the living room.

2. My mum works in an office.

3. Our dog plays in the garden.

4. Mary and I go to the cinema after school.

5. My dad repairs our car in the garage.

6. I go to school.

7. He finds his hamburgers in the fridge.

Station 2

What is it?

Name:

 task 1

Find the correct translations of the English questions and note them in your vocabulary book.

1. What's your name?	Was ist das?
2. What colour are your eyes?	Was ist deine Lieblingsfarbe?
3. What is this?	Was willst du?
4. What are you looking for?	Wie heißt du?
5. What is Peter's last name?	Was ist in der Schachtel?
6. What is your favourite colour?	Welche Farbe haben deine Augen?
7. What do you want?	Wie lautet Peters Nachname?
8. What's in the box?	Was / Wonach suchst du?

 task 2

Note the correct questions to the following answers.

1. It's my pencil.

   _____

2. My favourite food is pizza.

   _____

3. My mother's name is Mary.

   _____

4. I take a cup of coffee and a sandwich, please.

   _____

5. It is ten o'clock.

   _____

6. I am looking for the post office.

   _____

7. Our car is red.

   _____

Station 3

When is it?

Name:

task 1
Write down correct questions to the following answers.

1. It's on the 24th of December.

2. It is on Saturdays and Sundays.

3. It's on the 31st of December.

4. It's every year.

5. It's in the summer.

6. I do it in the afternoons.

7. It's in the winter.

8. I do it in the morning.

task 2
Write down the correct questions with "when" into your exercise book.

1. Sarah's birthday is on the 5th of July.
2. Peter comes home at ten o'clock.
3. Mary works every Saturday.
4. Sam's party is on Friday.
5. Jeremy and Sarah are coming home in the afternoon.
6. On Tuesdays, mum and dad go swimming in the evening.
7. Sarah and her best friends go to the cinema at eight o'clock.

Station 4

Why do you ask me?

Name:

task 1

Invent questions to the following answers.

1. Because I am too young. (cannot go to the disco)

   Why can't you _____

2. Because I have got a bad headache. (don't go to school)

   _____

3. Because it is raining. (stay at home)

   _____

4. Because mum isn't at home. (have lunch with the family)

   _____

5. Because my bike is broken. (take the bus)

   _____

6. Because I like music. (sing under the shower)

   _____

task 2

Tick the correct translations.

1. Warum bist du nicht in der Schule?
   - ☐ Why aren't you at school?
   - ☐ What are you doing at school?
   - ☐ Where is your school?

2. Ich weiß nicht warum.
   - ☐ I don't know where.
   - ☐ I don't know why.
   - ☐ I don't know who.

3. Warum ist es so kalt hier?
   - ☐ Where is it so cold?
   - ☐ Why is it so cold here?
   - ☐ When is it cold here?

4. Sie fragt mich warum.
   - ☐ She asks me where.
   - ☐ She asks me when.
   - ☐ She asks me why.

Station 5

How are you?

Name:

task 1
Translate the following sentences into English.

1. Wie alt bist du?
2. Wie geht es dir?
3. Wie lang ist der Zug?
4. Wie teuer ist es?
5. Wie viele Bücher hast du?
6. Wie alt ist dein Hund?
7. Wie nett!

task 2
Write down the words of the questions in the correct order.

1. old / how / you / are

2. many / cars / how / got / father / your / has

3. are / how / you

4. how / hamburgers / do / many / need / you

5. tall / am / I / how

6. nice / how / of / you

7. it / is / many / how / Christmas / till / months

Station 6

Who is it?

Name:

task 1
Write down the questions for the underlined persons in the sentences.

1. Peter likes Sally.

2. Mary sleeps in the living room.

3. The dog is under the table.

4. Marlon is going to have a party.

5. Tim is at school.

6. My mother is the best.

7. Dad is working in the garage.

8. My teacher is preparing our English test.

9. Sam has got an older sister.

10. Caroline is in London.

task 2

Write down the following questions in English and ask your partner.

1. Wer ist dein Lieblingssänger?
2. Wer ist dein bester Freund?
3. Wer sitzt jetzt neben dir?
4. Wer arbeitet jetzt mit dir?

Station 7

Question words I

Name:

task 1
Fill in the right questions word.

1. _____ is the ruler? where – how – who
2. _____ is this in English? how – what – who
3. _____ does she go? who – how – where
4. _____ do you say? what – where – how
5. _____ likes our English teacher? where – who – what
6. _____ do you live? who – where – when
7. _____ old is Mary? how – who – what
8. _____ time is it? how – who – what
9. _____ day is it today? why – what – how
10. _____ colour are your pencils? how – why – what

task 2
Cut out the memory® cards and mix them. Find the pairs of sentences and questions that go together. The one of you who finds most of the pairs is the winner of this game.

task 3
Fill in the right question words. The answers may help you.

1. _____ is your favourite hobby? – Tennis.
2. _____ old is your sister? – She is eleven.
3. _____ is John? – In the kitchen.
4. _____ can I do for you? – I need two melons and ten bananas.
5. _____ are you so tired? – Because my little baby sister cries all the time.
6. _____ is your best friend? – It's Marlon.
7. _____ are your pencils? – They are in my new pencil case.
8. _____ colour is your bike? – It's white.
9. _____ are you late? – Because I have got no watch.
10. _____ is your birthday? – It's on May 3rd.

Station 7

Memory® cards

Name:

Where are you?	I'm in the garden.	Who is your best friend?	My best friend is Sarah.
How old are you?	I'm ten.	Why is he late?	Because of his father.
Where is your mum?	She is in the kitchen.	Who are you?	I am Sam.
What is your favourite sport?	It's football.	Where does Sandra live?	She lives in my street.
Where are you from?	I'm from Berlin.	What is Peter's surname?	His surname is Walter.
What's your name?	My name is Sam.	When is your birthday?	It's on May 3rd.

Station 8

Question words II

Name: _____

 task 1

Fill in the right questions word and complete the rules.

"_____" is to ask about people.	_____ is the boy next to the door?
"_____" is to ask about places.	_____ is your house?
"_____" is to ask about time.	_____ does the film start?
"_____" is to ask for a reason.	_____ are you late today?
"_____" is to ask about the way you do something.	_____ do you spell this word?

 task 2

Ask for the underlined parts of the sentences. Use the question words from the chart.

1. Sally plays in her room.

   _____

2. Peter gets up at half past six in the morning.

   _____

3. Mrs. Miller gets to work by train.

   _____

4. Mary often goes to the cinema.

   _____

5. The kids in my class like ice cream.

   _____

6. Stephanie can't go to school because she's ill.

   _____

7. Peter and Sam read a book.

   _____

Station 9

Personal questions

Name:

 task
Answer the following questions.

1. What's your name?

    My name _____

2. How old are you?

    _____

3. Where are you from?

    _____

4. How are you today?

    _____

5. What's your mother's name?

    _____

6. How old is your dad?

    _____

7. Who is your best friend?

    _____

8. What's your favourite colour?

    _____

9. Who's your favourite singer?

    _____

10. What's your favourite book?

    _____

11. When were you born?

    _____

12. Why do you learn English?

    _____

Station 1

Articles

Name:

task 1
Decide if you need "a" or "an" to complete the sentences.

1. Peter is _____ good friend.
2. We meet our friends in _____ hour.
3. _____ good mark in English is very important.
4. Do you have _____ new teacher?
5. I have _____ old bike.
6. Sarah wants _____ nice birthday present.
7. Sam always writes _____ better mark than Tina.
8. Caroline and her father go on _____ trip to Australia.
9. We watch _____ American movie.
10. I am going to have _____ party on Saturday.

task 2
Fill the gaps with "a" or "an".

1. _____ old car
2. _____ big party
3. _____ orange jacket
4. _____ hotel room
5. _____ hour ago
6. _____ nice book
7. _____ overall
8. _____ apple
9. _____ yellow banana
10. _____ English book

Mixed up grammar topics

73

Station 2

The genitive

Name:

task 1
Write sentences about the things and whom they belong to. Start like this: This is ... These are ...

1. bike – Peter

2. pencil case – Sarah

3. house – the Millers

4. car – my family

5. dogs – Angie

6. hamster – Caroline

7. books – our teachers

8. room – Tom and Jerry

9. tests – our friends

task 2
Translate the following sentences into English by using the genitive.

1. Das ist das Haus der Brandys.

2. Das ist Marys Hund.

3. Das sind Mr. Millers Katzen.

4. Das ist das Auto unserer Eltern.

Station 3

A telephone call

Name: _____

 task
Put the dialogue in the right order and write it into your exercise book.

- Bye Sue, see you tomorrow at school.
- Hi Perry, it's Sue. How are you?
- Oh, what's the problem?
- Thanks a lot. See you. Bye.
- London 3583795038.
- I'm fine. Listen, Perry. I have got a big problem.
- Hi Sue. I am fine. And you?
- I can't take Jim for a walk today. Can you help?
- Yes, Sue. No problem. I love Jim.

Mixed up grammar topics

Station 4

Personal pronouns I

Name:

 task 1

Connect the right personal pronoun with a person/animal.

he	Sandra
she	Jenny and I
it	our budgie
we	Peter
they	Sam and Carol

 task 2

Cut out the cards, mix them and play the memory® game.
After your game write five sentences using the personal pronouns and the names of the game into your exercise book, e.g.: This is Tom. He is my best friend.

Sarah	she	Tom	he
my mum	she	Peer and Sam	they
Carol and I	we	my dad	he
the dog	it	the boys	they

Station 5

Personal pronouns II

Name: _____

task

Tick the right solutions to replace the underlined objects.

1. The teacher always gives <u>the students</u> homework.
   - ☐ me
   - ☐ them
   - ☐ you

2. I am reading a fairy tale to <u>my younger brother</u>.
   - ☐ her
   - ☐ us
   - ☐ him

3. The girls are talking to <u>Mrs. Miller</u>.
   - ☐ it
   - ☐ them
   - ☐ her

4. My brother is writing a letter to <u>grandma and grandpa</u>.
   - ☐ me
   - ☐ them
   - ☐ him

5. I know <u>the answer</u>.
   - ☐ she
   - ☐ her
   - ☐ it

6. Sandra is calling <u>her best friend Sue</u>.
   - ☐ her
   - ☐ him
   - ☐ me

7. Open <u>the door</u>, please.
   - ☐ it
   - ☐ them
   - ☐ us

8. Can you tell <u>these Japanese people</u> the way to the station, please?
   - ☐ you
   - ☐ them
   - ☐ us

9. The flowers are for <u>mum and me</u>.
   - ☐ him
   - ☐ us
   - ☐ you

10. Can you give <u>John</u> the photos, please?
    - ☐ her
    - ☐ him
    - ☐ us

Mixed up grammar topics

Station 6

Colours I

Name:

task 1

What colours are the different things? Write them down in English.

1. a snowman _____
2. a banana _____
3. an apple _____
4. a basketball _____
5. an egg _____

6. a tyre _____
7. a cactus _____
8. your eyes _____
9. leaves _____
10. a tree trunk _____

task 2

Write a short text about your classroom. Use a colour in every sentence.

Station 7

Colours II

Name:

task 1
Show the things in box 1 to a partner and let him tell you the colours of the things. Correct him/her, if necessary. Then let your partner show you the things in box 2 and tell him/her the colours of the things.

task 2
Now write down the colours of the things in the two boxes in whole sentences. Start your sentences like this: In box 1, there is a red …

1. _____
2. _____
3. _____
4. _____
5. _____
6. _____
7. _____
8. _____
9. _____
10. _____

Station 8

Body parts

Name:

task 1

Fill in the right English words.

[crossword grid]

Down:
1. Ohr
2. Nase
3. Bein
4. Haar
5. Zahn
6. Bauch
7. Auge
8. Arm

Across:
9. Fuß
10. Hand
11. Daumen
12. Schulter
13. Zeh
14. Rücken
15. Kopf
16. Lippe

task 2

Fill in the right word for every part of the body.

1.  _____
2.  _____
3. _____
4. _____
5.  _____

6. 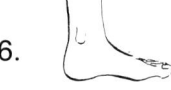 _____
7. _____
8.  _____
9. _____
10.  _____

Mixed up grammar topics

Station 9

Clothing

Name:

 task 1

Cut out the domino cards. Watch out: Don't separate the picture from the word, only separate the domino cards. Then play domino. Connect the right words and pictures to get a complete "clothing-snake".

 task 2

Translate the following sentences into English.

1. Meine Mutter kauft einen neuen Schal.

2. Sarah hat eine Bluse und eine Jacke an.

3. Ich kaufe eine neue Mütze.

4. Peter trägt eine Hose und einen gelben Pullover.

5. Jim trägt seine Badehose.

6. Mary und Sue mögen ihre neuen Röcke.

7. In meiner Klasse trägt niemand ein Kleid.

 task 3

Take your exercise book, draw a picture of one article of clothing and let your partner guess what it is. Then let your partner draw a picture and guess what he/she is drawing. Everybody should draw at least three articles of clothing.

Station 9

Domino cards

Name:

Mixed up grammar topics

trousers	*(pullover)*
pullover	*(cap)*
cap	*(jacket)*
jacket	*(shoes)*
shoes	*(socks)*
socks	*(scarf)*
scarf	*(coat)*
coat	*(skirt)*
skirt	*(blouse)*
blouse	*(dress)*
dress	*(trousers)*

Station 10

Asking the way

Name: _____

 task

Look at the map and describe the way to five different places to your partner.
He/She should tell you the way to the other five places afterwards.

Bus stop	School
	Station
Church	Mary's house	Tom's house
swimming pool	bakery	gym
	bucher's shop	

Mixed up grammar topics

Station 1: My day — page 10

task:

I <u>wake up</u> at six o'clock in the morning and <u>go</u> to the bathroom. There I <u>brush</u> my teeth, <u>wash</u> my face and <u>comb</u> my hair.

I <u>leave</u> the house at ten to seven. At a quarter past seven, I <u>arrive</u> at school. From half past seven till quarter to eight, we <u>have</u> breakfast together. The first lesson <u>starts</u> at eight o'clock. After the first lesson we <u>have</u> a small break of fifteen minutes. At half past nine, we <u>have</u> a big break of thirty minutes. At ten o'clock, the next lesson <u>begins</u>. At quarter to eleven, we <u>must</u> clean our classroom. After that, we <u>have</u> time to <u>relax</u>, to <u>talk</u> or to <u>play</u> table tennis. After lunch, we <u>do</u> different kinds of projects. We can <u>choose</u> between the wood working project, the photo or painting project and some sports.

At two o'clock, we <u>can</u> go home. Then I <u>do</u> my homework. After homework, I <u>meet</u> my friends, <u>play</u> outside or <u>watch</u> TV. We <u>eat</u> at eight o'clock when dad <u>comes</u> home. I <u>go</u> to bed at nine o'clock in the evening.

Station 2: What we do on Saturdays — page 11

task 1:

Individual solutions.

task 2:

1. On Saturdays, Sue does homework.
2. On Saturdays, Peter eats hamburgers.
3. On Saturdays, Peter gets up at ten o'clock.
4. On Saturdays, Sue watches TV.
5. On Saturdays, Sue makes breakfast.
6. On Saturdays, Peter goes to bed late.
7. On Saturdays, Sue meets friends.

Station 3: We don't and he doesn't — page 12

task 1:

1. Sarah doesn't write into her diary today.
2. Tom doesn't play with his friends in the garden.
3. The Millers don't watch TV very often.
4. Branda and Carol don't like their new English teacher.
5. Our cat doesn't like its food today.
6. My brother doesn't like homework.

task 2:

1. I don't like table tennis.
2. Sarah doesn't play tennis.
3. Peter and Tom don't like football.

Station 4: Do you like it? — page 13

task 1:

1. Do you like shirts? – Yes, I do.
2. Does he live in London? – Yes, he does.
3. Do the Millers like football? – Yes, they do.
4. Does Sally play the piano? – No, she doesn't.
5. Do I play tennis well? – No, you don't.
6. Do we speak English well? – Yes, we do.

task 2:

1. Does she do her homework every day?
2. Do they like swimming?
3. Does he like his computer game?
4. Do you eat hamburgers every day?
5. Does your mum help you with your homework?

Station 5: Are you happy? — page 14

task 1:

Individual solutions.

task 2:

1. Is he in your class?
2. Are they happy today?
3. Am I your best friend?
4. Are your parents at work today?

Station 6: What I always do — page 15

task 1:
always, sometimes, usually, never, today, every week, normally, often, this week

task 2:
Individual solutions.

task 3:
Individual solutions.

Station 7: Family members — page 16

task 1:
Mutter – mother
Vater – father
Schwester – sister
Bruder – brother
Großmutter – grandmother
Großvater – grandfather
Cousin/e – cousin
Onkel – uncle
Tante – aunt

task 2:
1. father
2. grandmother
3. aunt
4. sister
5. cousin
6. grandfather

task 3:
Individual solutions.

Station 8: About my family — page 17

task 1:
Individual solutions.

task 2:
Individual solutions.

Station 9: Relationships — page 18

task 2:
Individual solutions.

Station 10: I have got a nice room — page 20

task 1:
Individual solutions.

task 2:
1.–9. In his room, Peter has got a chair, a desk, a computer, a wardrobe, a bed, a sofa, shelves, a carpet, a poster.

Station 11: She hasn't got a sister — page 21

task 1:
Individual solutions.

task 2:
1. Have you got a cat? – Yes, I have.
2. Have they got a dog? – No, they haven't.
3. Has he got a younger brother? – No, he hasn't.
4. Has she got my book? – Yes, she has.
5. Have we got our homework? – Yes, we have.

Station 12: Rooms — page 22

task 2:
Individual solutions.

Station 13: Animals — page 23

task 2:
Individual solutions.

task 3:
Individual solutions.

Station 14: Pets — page 25

task 1:
Individual solutions.

task 2:
1. It's a dog.
2. It's a cat.
3. It's a hamster.
4. It's a budgie/parrot.
5. It's a fish.
6. It's a mouse.
7. It's a rabbit.

Station 1: I am playing football — page 27

task 1:
1. I am sitting on the sofa.
2. I am playing basketball with my friend.
3. I am helping my mum in the garden.
4. I am singing a song.
5. I am going for a walk with the dog.
6. I am learning for a vocabulary test.

task 2:
1. Look, Peter is playing in the garden with our dog.
2. The dog is running after the ball.
3. Now, Peter is coming into the house. He is going into the kitchen.
4. Mum and dad are sitting in the living room. They are watching TV.
5. At the moment, Peter's sister is learning for an English test on Monday.
6. Now, Peter is leaving again. He is taking his bike to ride to the football field.
7. The boys are playing football now.

Station 2: We aren't singing — page 28

task 1:
1. At the moment, the boy isn't playing tennis.
2. At the moment, the girl isn't dancing.
3. At the moment, the girl isn't playing the piano.
4. At the moment, the boy isn't reading.
5. At the moment, the boys aren't playing football.

task 2:
1. Peter isn't playing with his sister now. / At the moment, Peter isn't playing with his sister.
2. Mum and dad aren't watching TV now. / At the moment, mum and dad aren't watching TV.
3. Sarah isn't learning for her English test now. / At the moment, Sarah isn't learning for her English test.
4. Tom isn't playing football with his friends now. / At the moment, Tom isn't playing football with his friends.
5. The Millers aren't meeting their friends now. / At the moment, the Millers aren't meeting their friends.
6. Donna and Mary aren't going for a walk now. / At the moment, Donna and Mary aren't going for a walk.

Station 3: Are you talking to me now? — page 29

task 1:
1. Is he playing football now?
2. Is she going for a walk with the dog?
3. Are the trainers talking to their teams now?
4. Are the kids playing the piano at the moment?
5. Are you playing basketball right now?
6. Are you swimming at the moment?

task 2:
1. Are you learning English now?
2. Are you playing tennis at the moment?
3. Are you dreaming of a good mark in English?
4. Are you working with a partner now?
5. Are you looking out of the window at the moment?
6. Are you meeting friends now?
7. Are you doing your homework right now?
8. Are you drinking tea at the moment?

Station 4: Hobbies — page 30

task:
Individual solutions.

Station 5: My favourite hobby — page 31

task 1:
1. biking
2. watching TV
3. reading
4. cooking
5. jogging
6. playing
7. dancing
8. skiing
9. singing

task 2:
Individual solutions.

Station 6: In the free time — page 32

task:
1./2.
1. Mary is riding a bike.
2. Tom and Judy are talking on the phone.
3. Jonny is reading a book.
4. The class is playing volleyball.
5. Julia is writing a letter.
6. Anna is skiing.
7. Carol and Jim are dancing.
8. Sue and Carla are surfing.
9. Kevin is swimming.
10. David is playing tennis.
11. Alan is watching TV.
12. Frank and Toni are boxing.
13. Marilyn is listening to music.
14. Kate is riding a horse.
12. Lisa is playing a computer game/working on the computer.
13. Toby is playing football.

Station 7: Sports — page 33

task 1:
Sports: football, basketball, skating, skiing, athletics, badminton, ping-pong, riding, surfing, swimming, tennis, volleyball, windsurfing, cycling
Verbs: catch, shoot, swim, win, skate, beat, cycle, hit, kick, lose, practice, ride, throw, play
Places: ring, court, gym, stadium
People: swimmer, athlete, badminton player, basketball player, boxer, cyclist, football player, skater, surfer, tennis player, volleyball player, coach, trainer
Equipment: bat, skates, football, racket, skis, basket, ball, net, basketball

task 2:
1. You play football in a team of eleven men or women and you need a ball.
2. You play table tennis/ping-pong against another player on a table. You need a small white ball.
3. You play basketball in a team of five players and you need a ball. You must throw the ball into a basket.
4. When you do swimming, you are in the water and can move in it really quickly.
5. You play tennis against one other player or you play in a team of two against another team. You need a racket and a small yellow ball.

Station 8: My favourite sport — page 34

task 1:
1. Sam is playing football at the moment.
2. Mary is riding her horse now.
3. Thomas and Kevin are playing tennis in the garden right now.
4. Look, Jenny is swimming.
5. At the moment, the two teams are playing table tennis/ping-pong.

task 2:
1. John is playing tennis.
2. Tom is reading a book.
3. Carol and her sister are surfing.
4. Sam and Perry are boxing.
5. The girls in my class are playing volleyball.

task 3:
Individual solutions.

Station 1: School things — page 35

task 2:
1. Buch
2. Radiergummi
3. Füller
4. Lineal
5. Anspitzer
6. Schultasche
7. Mäppchen
8. Heft
9. Ordner/Hefter
10. Klebestift/Kleber
11. Filzstift
12. Bleistift

Station 2: Lessons — page 36

task 2:
Individual solutions.

Station 3: Our school — page 38

task:
Individual solutions.

Station 4: In our classroom — page 39

task 1 and 2:
1. There is a board in our classroom.
2. There are tables in our classroom.
3. There are chairs in our classroom.
4. There isn't a playstation in our classroom.
5. There are windows in our classroom.
6. There is a desk in our classroom.
7. There isn't a car in our classroom.
8. There aren't sofas in our classroom.
9. There isn't a toilet in our classroom.

Station 5: Where is what? — page 40

task 1:
1. My book is under the table.
2. The chair is behind the desk.
3. The pencil is in my pencil case.
4. The board is next to the door.
5. The pictures are on the wall.
6. Our exercise books are on the table.
7. The girls are sitting behind the boys in the classroom.

task 2:
1. The pencil case is on the book./The book is under the pencil case.
2. The pen is under the table.
3. The teacher is next to the board.
4. The rubber is on the chair.
5. The girl is behind the table.
6. The ruler and the pencils are in the pencil case.

Station 6: Classroom discourse — page 41

task:
1. Könnten Sie das bitte noch einmal sagen?
   Could you say it again, please?
2. Könnten Sie das bitte an die Tafel schreiben?
   Could you write it on the board, please?
3. Entschuldigung, ich habe meine Hausaufgaben nicht gemacht.
   Sorry, I haven't done my homework.
4. Was haben wir auf?
   What's the homework?
5. Was heißt ... auf Deutsch/auf Englisch?
   What's ... in German/in English?
6. Was bedeutet ...?
   What does ... mean?
7. Könnten Sie mir bitte helfen?
   Could you help me, please?
8. Entschuldigung, dass ich zu spät komme.
   I'm sorry I'm late.
9. Entschuldigung, ich verstehe das nicht.
   Sorry, I don't understand this.

Station 7: In the gym — page 42

task 1:
1. The ball is in my hand.
2. The players stand in front of the goal.
3. The teacher always stands behind the line.
4. The school bags are in the changing stall (Umkleidekabine).
5. You can see our points on the chart.
6. The rackets are next to/under the balls.
7. We sit on the floor and talk to each other.
8. My shoes are next to/under the chair.

Station 8: The new teacher — page 43

task 2:
1. His name is Mr. Althaus.
2. Sarah asks the first questions.
3. Mary wants to know how old Mr. Athaus's children are.
4. Yes, he has a boy and two girls.
5. Because his wife and Mr. Althaus both have a new job in London.
6. The class has to write a test.

Station 1: I am going to have a party — page 44

task 1:
1. Sarah and I are going to have a party tomorrow.
2. My best friend Sally is going to come, too.
3. Peter is going to help me with the hamburgers.
4. Our parents are going to prepare the garage for the party.
5. On Saturday, my best friend Carol is going to have her birthday party.
6. I am going to go there at seven o'clock.
7. My brother Terry and his friend James are going to come with me.
8. On Sunday, we are going to sleep long, I think.

task 2:
1. The kids are going to go to the supermarket.
2. The kids are going to buy fruits.
3. The kids are going to make a salad.
4. The kids are going to bring tables and chairs into the garage.
5. The kids are going to prepare the music.

Station 2: I am not going to do all this — page 45

task 1:
1. I am not/I'm not going to go swimming tomorrow morning.
2. Dad and I are not/aren't going to play the piano.
3. Peter and I are not/aren't going to buy a present for grandma.
4. I am not/I'm not going to take the dog for a walk.
5. I am not/I'm not going to read a good book in the afternoon.
6. Mum and I are not/aren't going to prepare the Christmas tree.

task 2:

Individual solutions.

Station 3: Are you going to help me?
page 46

task 1:
1. Are you going to help me?
2. Is your mother going to buy everything for the party?
3. Is your brother going to make music?
4. Is Sarah going to come, too?
5. Are we going to play funny games?
6. Is your dad going to help you with the hamburgers?

task 2:
1. Are you going to have fun?
2. Is she going to eat salad?
3. Am I going to dance with you?
4. Are they going to sleep early?

Station 4: The shopping list
page 47

task 2:
1. Perry is going to have a party tonight.
2. No, she isn't going to go there alone. Perry is going to come with her.
3. Peter and Jim are going to come to the supermarket, too.
4. Perry's mum is going to prepare the drinks for the party.
5. The kids are going to take the bus at two o'clock.
6. Perry's mum is going to give the shopping list to the kids before they leave the house.

Station 5: Food and drinks
page 48

task 1:
Pepper, lettuce, tomatoes, cheese, a spoon, onions, oranges, meat, a knife, a bowl, pears, buns, lemons, a plate, kiwis, bananas, apples, grapes, melon, sugar, pineapple

task 2:
Individual solutions.

Station 6: An invitation snake
page 49

task:
Please, come to my birthday party on Friday, 6th of September. The party starts at seven o'clock! Peter.

Station 7: My party
page 50

task 1:
1. I am/I'm going to buy hamburgers.
2. I am/I'm going to bring tables and chairs into the garage.
3. I am/I'm going to invite friends.
4. I am/I'm going to buy new CDs.
5. I am/I'm going to ask my parents for help.
6. I am/I'm going to call some friends for help.

task 2:
Individual solutions.

Station 8: The new party outfit — page 51

task 1:

Costumer: Good afternoon.
Salesperson: Good afternoon. Can I help you?
Costumer: Yes, please. I have a party on Saturday and need new trousers.
Salesperson: Here you are, size eight.
Costumer: Thanks. I try them on.
Salesperson: Do they fit? Do you like the colour?
Costumer: Yes, they fit, but I don't like them in blue.
Salesperson: What about the white trousers?
Costumer: Yes, they are nice. I need a new tee shirt, too.
Salesperson: What size and colour, please?
Costumer: Size s, please. And I would like it in black.
Salesperson: Here you are. Does it fit?
Costumer: Yes, thank you. How much is it?
Salesperson: The tee shirt is 20 Pounds. It looks good. Do you want to take the things?
Costumer: Yes, I do.
Salesperson: Thank you very much.
Costumer: Bye bye.
Salesperson: Bye bye.

Station 1: Numbers from 1 to 100 — page 52

task 1:

three, twenty-one, thirty-nine, seventeen, eleven, forty-four, fifty-three, sixty-eight, seventy, eighty-two, ninety-nine, one hundred, thirteen, ninety-two, twelve, fifty-nine, seventy-five, thirty, nine, forty-eight, sixty, five, three, eighty-eight

task 3:

Individual solutions.

Station 2: Numbers from 100 to 1 000 — page 54

task 1:

320 — Three hundred twenty
490 — Four hundred ninety
102 — One hundred two
519 — Five hundred nineteen
677 — Six hundred seventy-seven
723 — Seven hundred twenty-three
891 — Eight hundred ninety-one
999 — Nine hundred ninety-nine
1000 — One thousand

task 2:

Individual solutions.

Station 3: Ordinal numbers — page 55

task 1:

Number	Ordinal Number	Short form
1	one	first	1st
2	two	second	2nd
3	three	third	3rd
5	five	fifth	5th
8	eight	eighth	8th
10	ten	tenth	10th
21	twenty-one	twenty-first	21st
33	thirty-three	thirty-third	33rd
40	forty	fortieth	40th
79	seventy-nine	seventy-ninth	79th
100	one hundred	one hundredth	100th

task 2:

1. Mum's birthday is on the 3rd / third of December.
2. Dad's birthday is on the 21st / twenty-first of May.
3. Peter's birthday is on the 1st / first of January.
4. Sarah's birthday is on the 2nd / second of June.
5. Grandma's birthday is on the 31st / thirty-first of August.
6. Grandpa's birthday is on the 5th / fifth of July.

Station 4: What's the time, please? — page 56

task 1:
Individual solutions.

task 2:

Station 5: It's ten o'clock now — page 58

task 1:
Individual solutions.

task 2:
It's a quarter to four.
It's half past four.
It's five past seven.
It's nine o'clock.
It's a quarter to one.
It's a quarter past six.
It's ten to eight.
It's one o'clock.
It's twenty to three.
It's ten past five.
It's six past three.
It's thirteen minutes to three.
It's half past one.
It's half past three.
It's nine past eight.
It's a quarter to five.
It's three past seven.
It's ten o'clock.
It's midnight/It's twelve o'clock.

Station 6: My day – telling the time — page 59

task 1:
1. At eight o'clock, Sarah goes to school.
2. At a quarter past one, Sarah arrives at home.
3. At half past two, Sarah has lunch.
4. At four o'clock, Sarah does her homework.
5. At a quarter to six, Sarah watches TV.
6. At a quarter past seven, Sarah eats with her family.
7. At half past eight, Sarah takes a shower.
8. At nine o'clock, Sarah goes to bed.

task 2:
Individual solutions.

Station 7: My week — page 60

task 1:
1. On Mondays, I always go swimming.
2. On Tuesdays and Wednesdays, I have piano lessons.
3. On Thursdays, I meet my friends after school.
4. On Fridays, I usually do all my homework and then I go for a walk with the dog.
5. On Saturdays, I sleep long. In the afternoons, we visit my grandparents.
6. On Sundays, I ride my horse and sometimes I meet my friends.

task 2:
Individual solutions.

Station 8: British money — page 61

task:

£ 1	one pound
£ 13	thirteen pounds
£ 4	four pounds
£ 8.90	eight pounds ninety
40p	forty pence
1p	one penny

£ 6.45	six pounds forty-five
45p	forty-five pence
£ 2.90	two pounds ninety
£ 100	one hundred pounds
55p	fifty-five pence
15p	fifteen pence
£ 2.40	two pounds forty
£ 3.30	three pounds thirty

Station 9: A month's quiz — page 62

task 1:
1. April, June, September, November
2. January, March, May, July, August, October, December
3. February
4. June, July, August
5. December, January, February
6. April, May, June, July, August, September
7. May
8. January, February, May, July

task 2:
Individual solutions.

Station 1: Where is it? — page 63

task 1:
1. 2, 2. 6, 3. 1, 4. 3, 5. 5, 6. 4

task 2:
1. Where do you do your homework?
2. Where does your mum work?
3. Where does your dog play?
4. Where do you and Mary go after school?
5. Where does your dad repair your car?
6. Where do you go?
7. Where does he find his hamburgers?

Station 2: What is it? — page 64

task 1:
1. What's your name? Wie heißt du?
2. What colour are your eyes? Welche Farbe haben deine Augen?
3. What is this? Was ist das?
4. What are you looking for? Was / Wonach suchst du?
5. What is Peter's last name? Wie lautet Peters Nachname?
6. What is your favourite colour? Was ist deine Lieblingsfarbe?
7. What do you want? Was willst du?
8. What's in the box? Was ist in der Schachtel?

task 2:
1. What is it?
2. What's your favourite food?
3. What's your mother's name?
4. What do you take?
5. What time is it?
6. What are you looking for?
7. What colour is your car?

Station 3: When is it? — page 65

task 1:
1. When is Christmas?
2. When is the weekend?
3. When is New Year's Eve?
4.–8. Individual solutions.

task 2:
1. When is Sarah's birthday?
2. When does Peter come home?
3. When does Mary work?
4. When is Sam's party?
5. When are Jeremy and Sarah coming home?
6. When do mum and dad go swimming in the evening?
7. When do Sarah and her best friends go to the cinema?

Station 4: Why do you ask me? — page 66

task 1:
1. Why can't you go to the disco?
2. Why don't you go to school?
3. Why do you stay at home?
4. Why don't you have lunch with the family?
5. Why do you take the bus?
6. Why do you sing under the shower?

task 2:
1. Why aren't you at school?
2. I don't know why.
3. Why is it so cold here?
4. She asks me why.

Station 5: How are you? — page 67

task 1:
1. How old are you?
2. How are you?
3. How long is the train?
4. How much is it? / How expensive is it?
5. How many books have you got / do you have?
6. How old is your dog?
7. How nice!

task 2:
1. How old are you?
2. How many cars has your father got?
3. How are you?
4. How many hamburgers do you need?
5. How tall am I?
6. How nice of you!
7. How many months is it till Christmas?

Station 6: Who is it? — page 68

task 1:
1. Who likes Sally?
2. Who sleeps in the living room?
3. Who is under the table?
4. Who is going to have a party?
5. Who is at school?
6. Who is the best?
7. Who is working in the garage?
8. Who is preparing our English test?
9. Who has got an older sister?
10. Who is in London?

task 2:
1. Who is your favourite singer?
2. Who is your best friend?
3. Who is sitting next to you now?
4. Who is working with you now?

Station 7: Question words I — page 69

task 1:
1. Where is the ruler?
2. What is this in English?
3. Where does she go?
4. What do you say?
5. Who likes our English teacher?
6. Where do you live?
7. How old is Mary?
8. What time is it?
9. What day is it today?
10. What colour are your pencils?

task 3:
1. What is your favourite hobby?
2. How old is your sister?
3. Where is John?
4. What can I do for you?
5. Why are you so tired?
6. Who is your best friend?
7. Where are your pencils?
8. What colour is your bike?
9. Why are you late?
10. When is your birthday?

Station 8: Question words II — page 71

task 1:

"Who" is to ask about people.	Who is the boy next to the door?
"Where" is to ask about places.	Where is your house?
"When" is to ask about time.	When does the film start?
"Why" is to ask for a reason.	Why are you late today?
"How" is to ask about the way you do something.	How do you spell this word?

task 2:
1. Where does Sally play?
2. When does Peter get up?
3. How does Mrs. Miller get to work?
4. Where does Mary often go?
5. What do the kids in your class like?
6. Why can't Stephanie go to school?
7. What do Peter and Sam read?

Station 9: Personal questions — page 72

task:
Individual solutions.

Station 1: Articles — page 73

task 1:
1. Peter is a good friend.
2. We meet our friends in an hour.
3. A good mark in English is very important.
4. Do you have a new teacher?
5. I have an old bike.
6. Sarah wants a nice birthday present.
7. Sam always writes a better mark than Tina.
8. Caroline and her father go on a trip to Australia.
9. We watch an American movie.
10. I am going to have a party on Saturday.

task 2:
1. an old car
2. a big party
3. an orange jacket
4. a hotel room
5. an hour ago
6. a nice book
7. an overall
8. an apple
9. a yellow banana
10. an English book

Station 2: The genitive — page 74

task 1:
1. This is Peter's bike.
2. This is Sarah's pencil case.
3. This is the Milllers' house.
4. This is my family's car.
5. These are Angie's dogs.
6. This is Caroline's hamster.
7. These are our teachers' books.
8. This is Tom and Jerry's room.
9. These are our friends' tests.

task 2:
1. This is the Brandys' house.
2. This is Mary's dog.
3. These are Mr. Miller's cats.
4. This is our parents' car.

Station 3: A telephone call — page 75

task:
1. London 3583795038.
2. Hi Perry, it's Sue. How are you?
3. Hi Sue. I am fine. And you?
4. I'm fine. Listen, Perry. I have got a big problem.
5. Oh, what's the problem?
6. I can't take Jim for a walk today. Can you help?
7. Yes, Sue. No problem. I love Jim.
8. Thanks a lot. See you. Bye.
9. Bye Sue, see you tomorrow at school.

Station 4: Personal pronouns I — page 76

task 1:
- he — Peter
- she — Sandra
- it — our budgie
- we — Jenny and I
- they — Sam and Carol

task 2:
Individual solutions.

Station 5: Personal pronouns II — page 77

task:
1. them
2. him
3. her
4. them
5. it
6. her
7. it
8. them
9. us
10. him

Station 6: Colours I — page 78

task 1:
1. white
2. yellow
3. red/green
4. orange
5. white
6. black
7. green
8. Individual solution.
9. green
10. brown

task 2:
Individual solutions.

Station 7: Colours II — page 79

task 1 and 2:
Individual solutions.

Station 8: Body parts — page 80

task 1:

Down:
1. ear
2. nose
3. leg
4. hair
5. tooth
6. stomach
7. eye
8. arm

Across:
9. foot
10. hand
11. thumb
12. shoulder
13. toe
14. back
15. head
16. lip

task 2:
1. arm
2. eye
3. hair
4. head
5. leg
6. foot
7. nose
8. mouth
9. ear
10. hand

Station 9: Clothing — page 81

task 2:
1. My mother buys/is buying a new scarf.
2. Sarah wears/is wearing a blouse and a jacket.
3. I buy/am buying a new cap.
4. Peter wears/is wearing a pair of/some trousers and a yellow pullover.
5. Jim wears/is wearing his swimming trunks.
6. Mary and Sue like there new skirts.
7. In my class, nobody wears/is wearing a dress.

task 3:
Individual solutions.

Station 10: Asking the way — page 83

task:
Individual solutions.